KEV's
QUICKSTART
UKE

T0081727

UKULELE
CHRISTMAS
SONGS

By KEV - Kevin Rones

ISBN 978-1-57424-287-4
SAN 633-8022

Cover, illustrations, design & music by KEV.

CENTERSTREAM®

TABLE OF CONTENTS

Away in the Manger

Traditional

Arranged by KEV

A- way in a man- ger, no crib for a

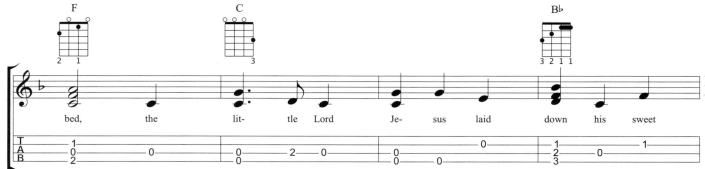

bed, the lit- tle Lord Je- sus laid down his sweet

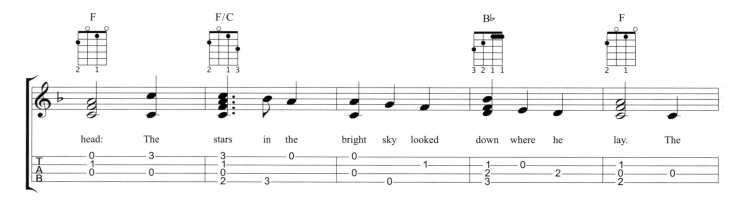

head: The stars in the bright sky looked down where he lay. The

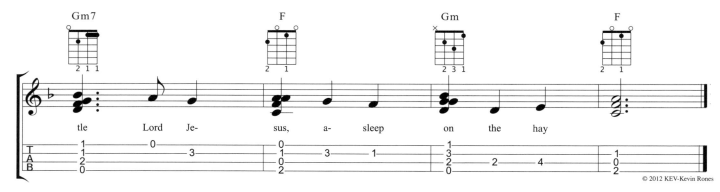

tle Lord Je- sus, a- sleep on the hay

© 2012 KEV-Kevin Rones

Carol of the Bells

Traditional

Arranged by KEV

God Rest Ye Merry Gentlemen
Traditional
Arranged by KEV

God rest ye mer- ry, gent- le- men Let no- thing you dis- may Re-

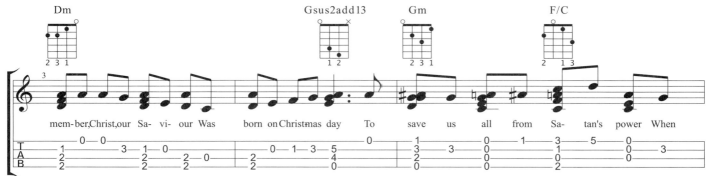

mem- ber, Christ, our Sa- vi- our Was born on Christmas day To save us all from Sa- tan's power When

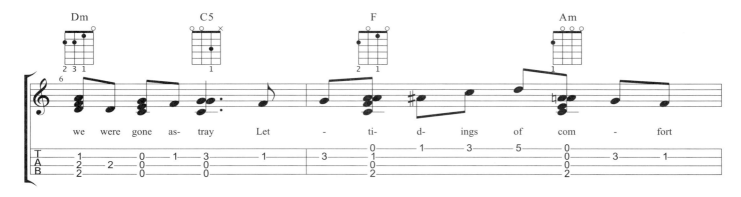

we were gone as- tray Let - ti- d- ings of com - fort

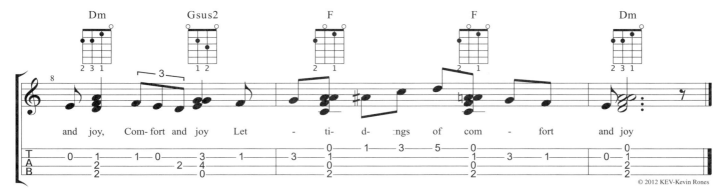

and joy, Com- fort and joy Let - ti- d- ings of com - fort and joy

Hark The Herald Angels Sing

Traditional   Arranged by KEV

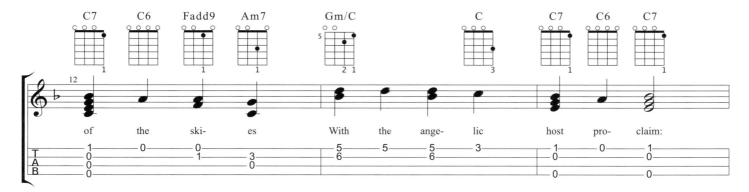

of the ski- es   With the ange- lic   host pro- claim:

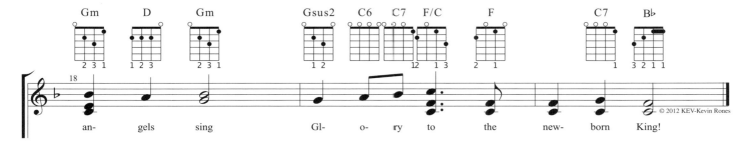

Chri-   st   is born   in   Beth- le-   hem   Hark!   The   her- ald

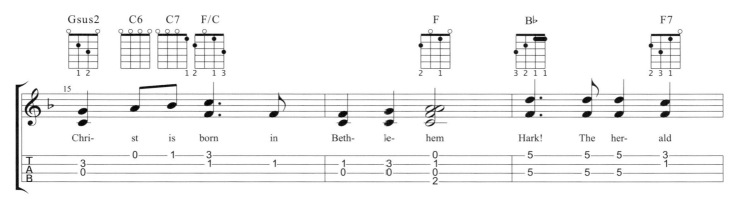

an-   gels   sing   Gl-   o-   ry   to   the   new- born   King!

© 2012 KEV-Kevin Rones

Jingle Bells

Traditional

Arranged by KEV

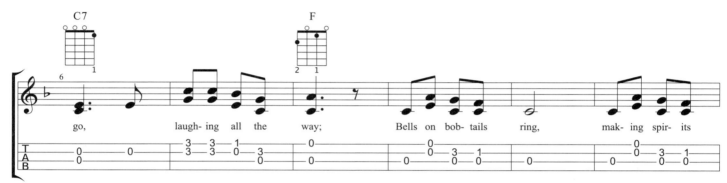

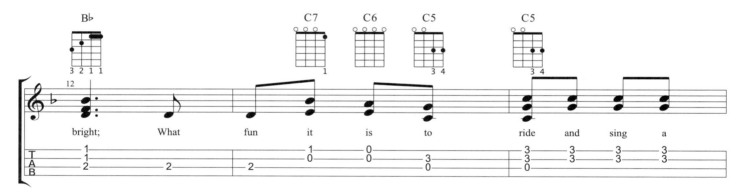

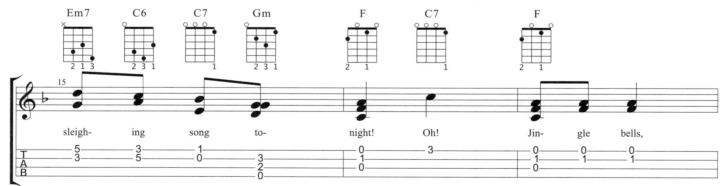

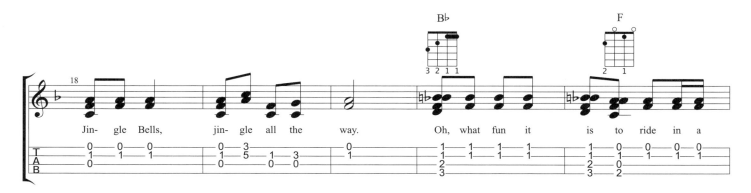

Jin- gle Bells, jin- gle all the way. Oh, what fun it is to ride in a

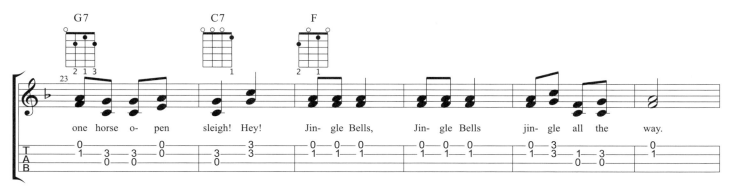

one horse o- pen sleigh! Hey! Jin- gle Bells, Jin- gle Bells jin- gle all the way.

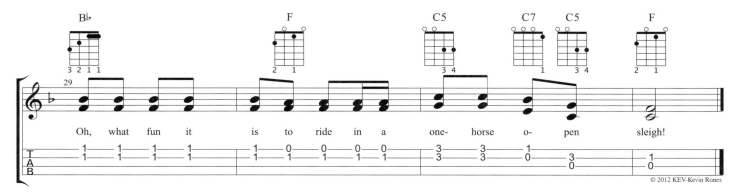

Oh, what fun it is to ride in a one- horse o- pen sleigh!

Joy To The World
Traditional

Arranged by KEV

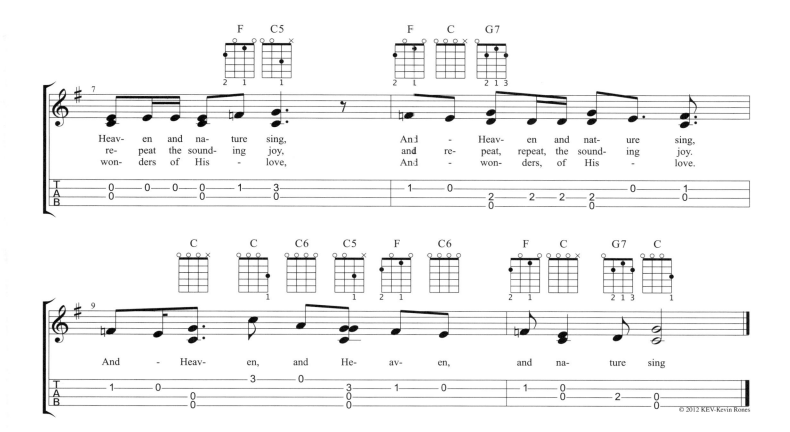

O Come All Ye Faithful

Traditional

Arranged by KEV

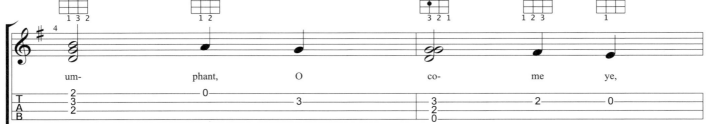

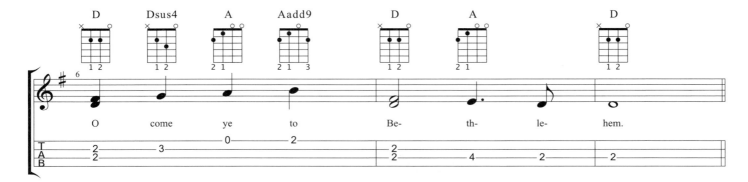

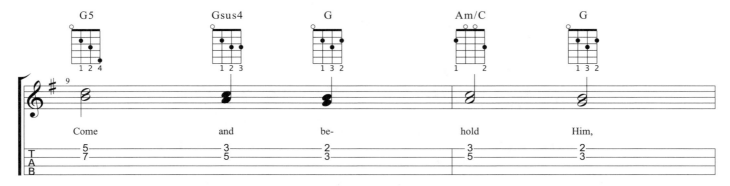

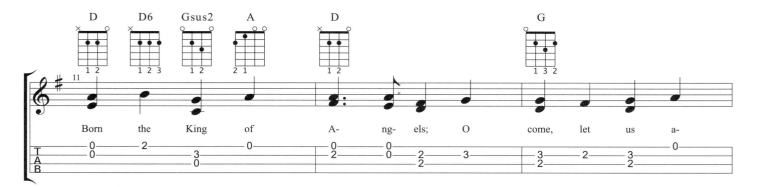

Born   the   King   of   A-   ng-els;   O   come,   let   us   a-

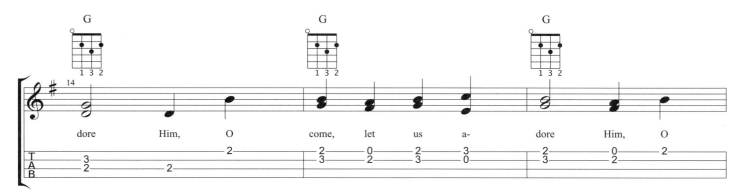

dore   Him,   O   come,   let   us   a-   dore   Him,   O

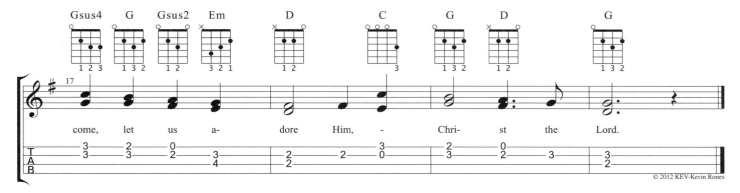

come,   let   us   a-   dore   Him,   -   Chri-   st   the   Lord.

O Christmas Tree

Traditional

Arranged by KEV

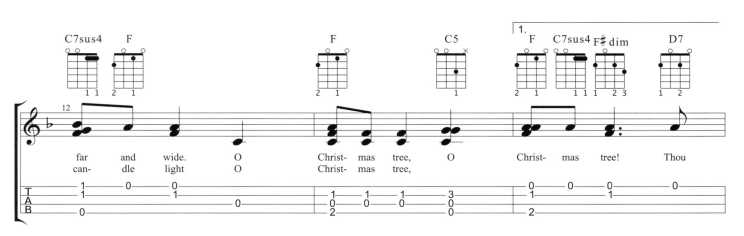

far   and   wide.   O   Christ- mas tree,   O   Christ- mas tree! Thou
can-   dle   light   O   Christ- mas tree,

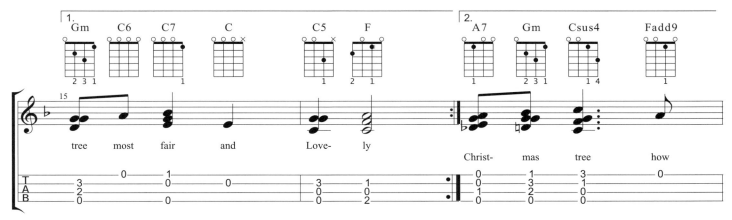

tree   most   fair   and   Love- ly   Christ- mas tree   how

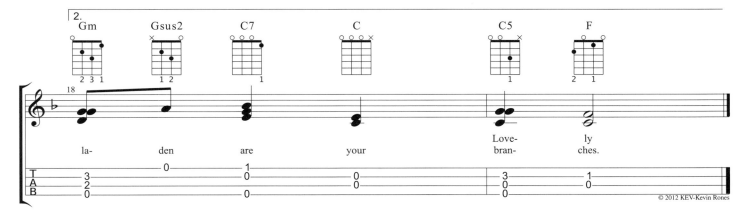

la-   den   are   your   Love- ly
                                            bran- ches.

The First Noel

Traditional

Arranged by KEV

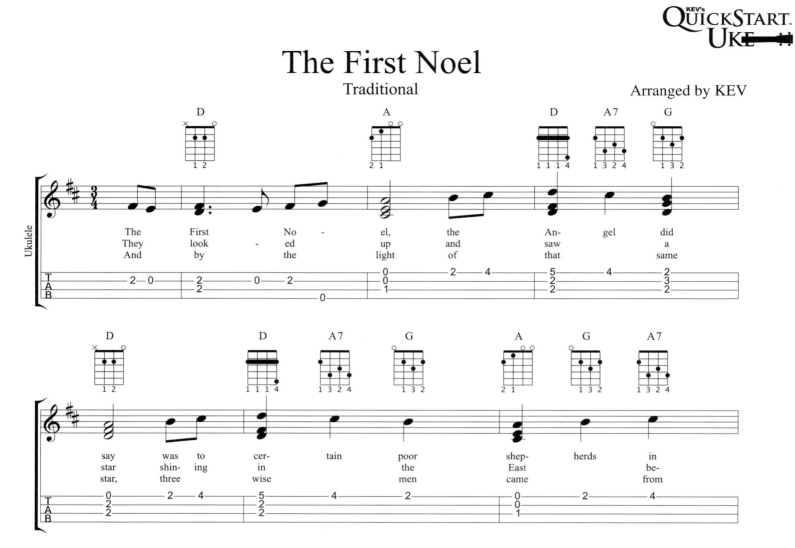

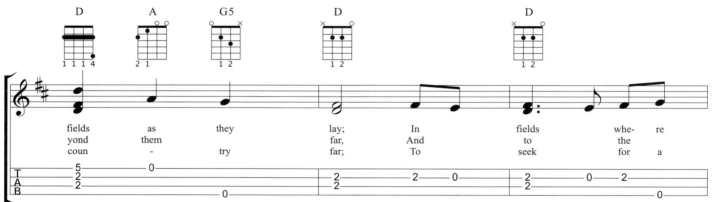

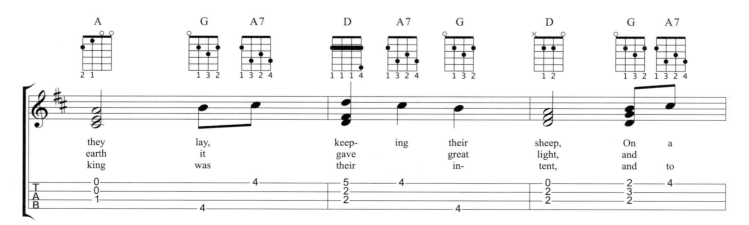

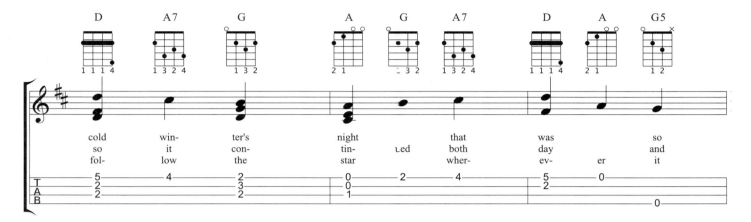

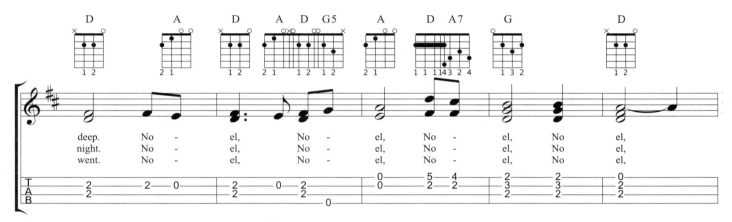

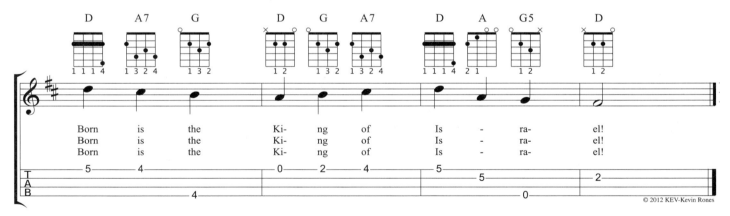

We Three Kings of Orient Are

Traditional

Arranged by KEV

Refrain

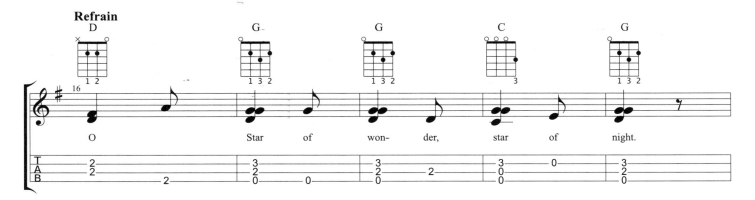

O Star of won- der, star of night.

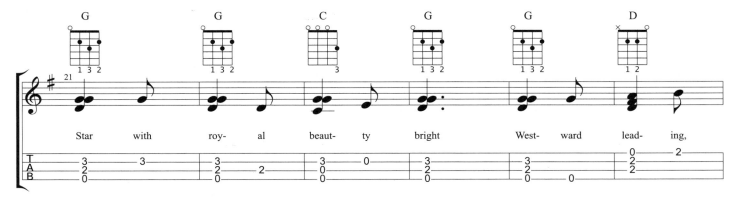

Star with roy- al beaut- ty bright West- ward lead- ing,

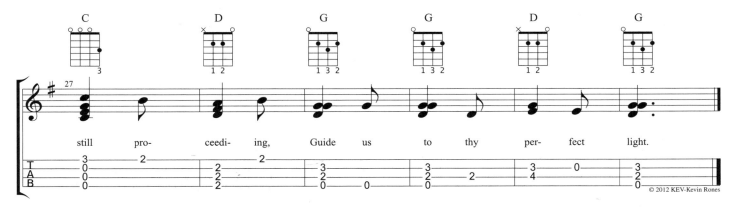

still pro- ceedi- ing, Guide us to thy per- fect light.

We Wish You A Merry Christmas

Traditional

Arranged by KEV

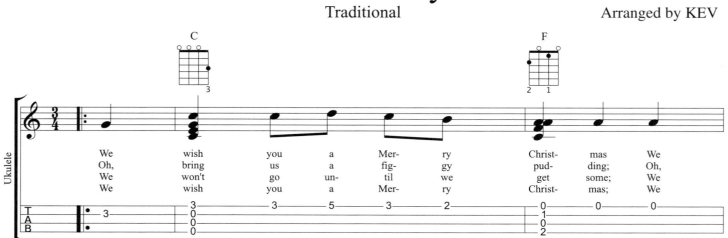

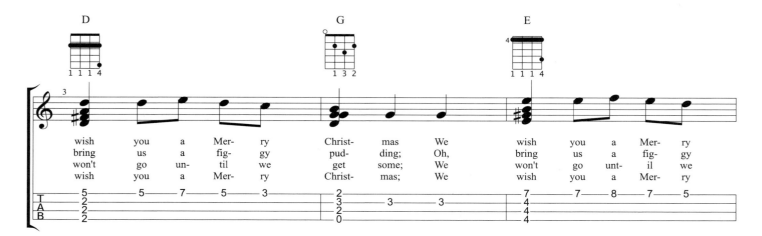

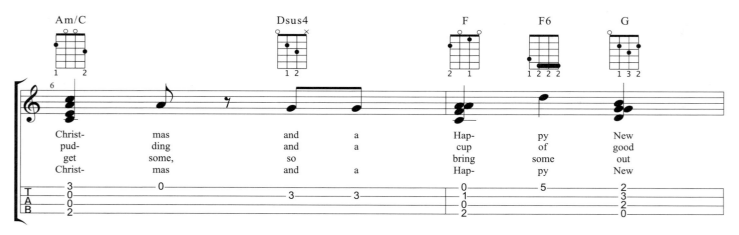

Chorus

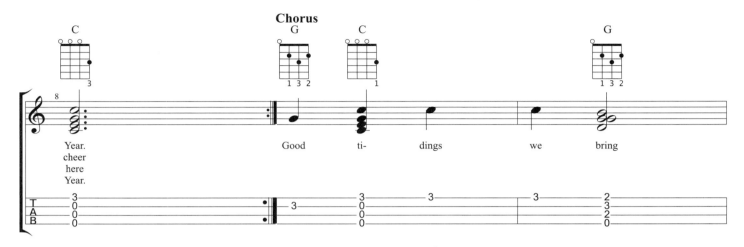

Year.
cheer
here
Year.

Good ti- dings we bring

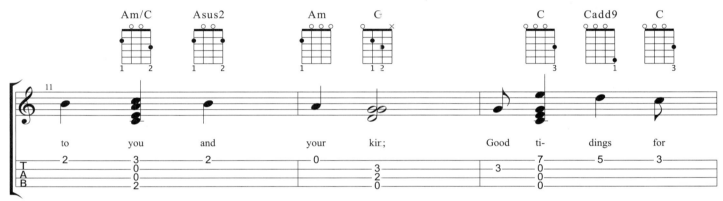

to you and your kin; Good ti- dings for

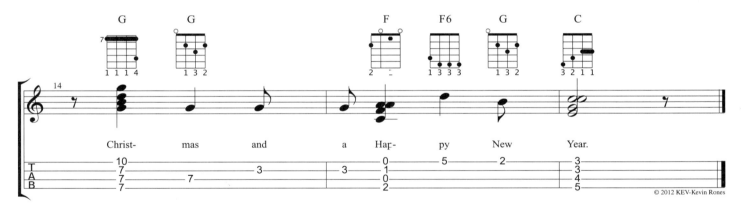

Christ- mas and a Hap- py New Year.

Away in a Manger

```
F         |        Bb       F
Away in a manger no crib for a bed
   C7              Gm              F
The little Lord Jesus laid down His sweet head
      F                    Bb              F
The stars in the sky looked down where He lay
     Gm      F      Gm      C7 F
The little Lord Jesus a-sleep on the hay

      F                Bb          F
The cattle are lowing the poor baby wakes
     C7               Gm        F
But little Lord Jesus no crying He makes
 F                       Bb              F
I love Thee Lord Jesus  look down from the sky
     Gm      F      Gm      C7 F
And stay by my cradle till morning is nigh
```

God Rest Ye Merry Gentlemen

```
   Dm                                        A
God rest ye merry, gentlemen; Let nothing you dis-may;
  Dm                                         A
Re-member Christ our Savior was born on Christmas Day
  Gm  C6     F     C6        Dm    C6    C5
To save us all from Satan's pow'r, when we were gone a-stray.
```

Chorus:
```
   F      Am       Dm            C5
 Let tidings of comfort and joy, comfort and joy;
   F      F        Dm
 Let tidings of com-fort and joy.
```

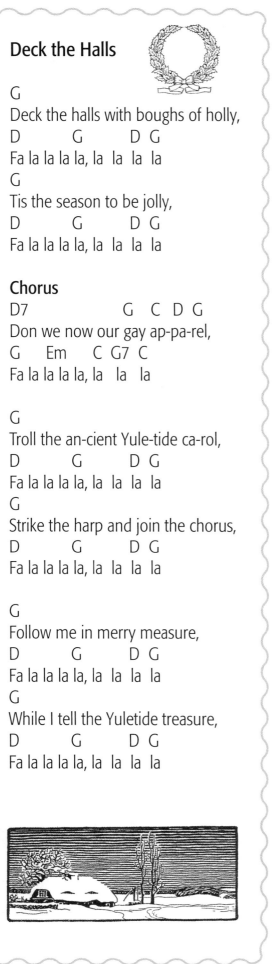

Deck the Halls

```
G
Deck the halls with boughs of holly,
D       G        D  G
Fa la la la la, la  la  la  la
G
Tis the season to be jolly,
D       G        D  G
Fa la la la la, la  la  la  la
```

Chorus
```
D7                G  C  D  G
Don we now our gay ap-pa-rel,
G   Em      C  G7  C
Fa la la la la, la  la  la
```

```
G
Troll the an-cient Yule-tide ca-rol,
D       G        D  G
Fa la la la la, la  la  la  la
G
Strike the harp and join the chorus,
D       G        D  G
Fa la la la la, la  la  la  la
```

```
G
Follow me in merry measure,
D       G        D  G
Fa la la la la, la  la  la  la
G
While I tell the Yuletide treasure,
D       G        D  G
Fa la la la la, la  la  la  la
```

Hark The Herald Angels Sing

F
Hark the herald angels sing
C   C7 F   Am7 F
Glory to the new born King
F
Peace on earth and mercy mild
C   G   C
God an sinners re-con-ciled

F/C   F C7 C6   Am7
Joyful all ye na-tions ri-se
F/C   F   C7 C6   Am7
Join the tri-umph of the ski-es

Gm   F Gm F   Gm
With angel-ic host pro-claim
Gsus2 C6 C7 F/C F   Gm F
Chri - st is born in Beth- le- hem

Bb   F Gm D7 Gm
Hark the her-ald an - gels sing
Gsus2 C6   Gm F/C F   C7   F
Gl - o - ry to   the new born King

Jingle Bells

F   Bb
Dashing through the snow, in a one horse open sleigh
Gm   C7   F
O'er the fields we go, laughing all the way.
F   Bb
Bells on bobtail ring, making spirits bright.
Bb   C5   F
What fun it is to ride and sing a sleigh-ing song to-night!

C7   F
Oh! Jingle bells, jingle bells, jingle all the way.
Bb   F   C5
Oh what fun it is to ride in a one horse open sleigh.
F
Jingle bells, jingle bells, jingle all the way.
Bb   F   C   C7 Gm F
Oh what fun it is to ride in a one horse op - en sleigh.

Joy to the World!

C
Joy to the world, the Lord is come!
    F   G   C
Let earth re-ceive her King;
        C
Let every heart
          C
pre-pare Him room,
          C
And heaven and nature sing,
     G   G7
And heaven and nature sing,
          C   G7   C
And heaven, and heaven, and na-ture sing.

O Come All Ye Faithful

   G   D
O come, all ye faithful,
G   D
joyful and trium-phant;
    Em   D
O come ye, O come ye
   D   A7 D
to Beth-el-ehem.
G   D7
Come and be-hold Him,
 G   Em   D
Born the King of an-gels

Chorus

   G
O come, let us adore Him;
   G
O come, let us adore Him;
   G   D C
O come, let us a-dore Him,
G   D7   G
Chri - st the Lord!

O Christmas Tree

```
F              Gm  F
O Christ-mas tree, O  Christ-mas tree!
    Gm            C7 Gm  F
Thou tree most fair and love-ly
 F             Gm  F
O Christ-mas tree, O  Christ-mas tree!
    Gm            C7 Gm  F
Thou tree most fair and love-ly!
```

```
C  F/C  F D  C        Gm
The sight of thee at Christ-mas-tide
Gm            C  C7    F
spreads hope and glad-ness far and wide.
 F             Gm  F
O Christ-mas tree, O  Christ-mas tree!
    Gm            C7 Gm  F
Thou tree most fair and love-ly!
```

The First Noel

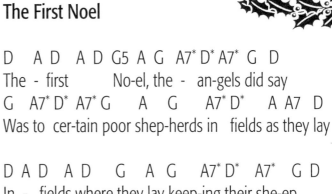

```
D   A D   A D G5 A G  A7* D* A7*  G  D
The - first     No-el, the - an-gels did say
G  A7* D* A7* G   A  G    A7* D*   A  A7 D
Was to cer-tain poor shep-herds in  fields as they lay

D A D   A D   G  A G   A7* D*  A7*  G  D
In - fields where they lay keep-ing their she-ep,
 G A7* D*  A7* G   A   G A7* D*  A  G  D
On a  cold win-ters night - that was - so deep

D      A    G   D
Noel, No-el, Noel, Noel
D   A7* G  A  G A7* D*  A  G D
Born is the Ki-ng of Is - r - a - el
```

* use alternate form of chord. See chord reference page.

We Three Kings of Orient Are

```
Em            B   Em
We three kings of Orient are;
Em            B       Em
Bearing gifts, we traverse a-far,
Em       D    G
Field and fountain, moor and mountain,
Am       B    Em
Following yonder star.
```

```
Refrain
 D G           C   G
 O, star of wonder, star of night,
 G           C    G
 Star with royal beauty bright,
 Em    D    C    D
 Westward leading, still pro-ceeding,
 G           C    G
 Guide us to thy perfect light.
```

We Wish You A Merry Christmas

```
C                  F
We wish you a Merry Christmas.
    D           G7
We wish you a Merry Christmas..
    E           Am         F Dm G   C
We wish you a Merry Christmas and a Hap-py  New Year.
```

Chorus

```
G    C     G       Am/C Asus2 Am G
Good tidings we bring to you   and   your kin..
G    C     G            F Dm G   C
Good tidings for Christmas and a Hap-py New Year.

C                  F
Now, bring us a figgy pudding..
    D           G7
Oh, bring us a figgy pudding..
    E           Am         F Dm G   C
Oh, bring us a figgy pudding and a cup of  good cheer.
```

KEV's
QUICKSTART.
UKE

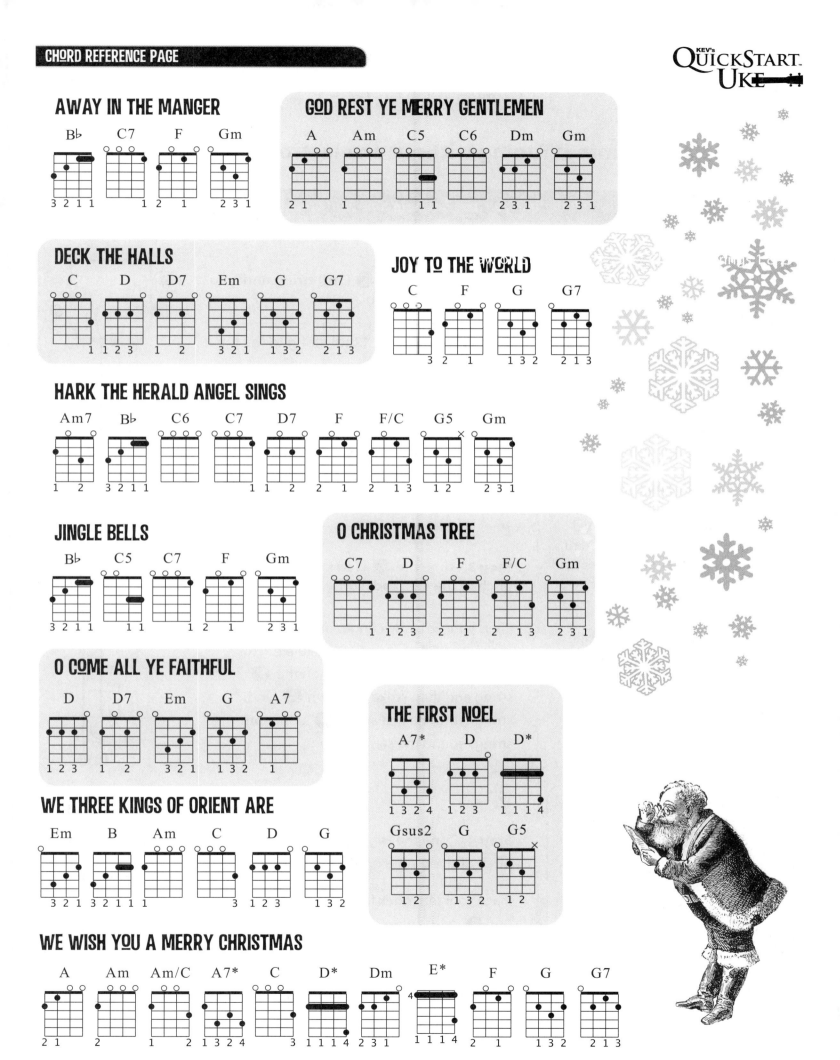

AWAY IN THE MANGER

GOD REST YE MERRY GENTLEMEN

DECK THE HALLS

JOY TO THE WORLD

HARK THE HERALD ANGEL SINGS

JINGLE BELLS

O CHRISTMAS TREE

O COME ALL YE FAITHFUL

THE FIRST NOEL

WE THREE KINGS OF ORIENT ARE

WE WISH YOU A MERRY CHRISTMAS

Tuning Your Ukulele

C tuning (High G) - G C E A

Relative Tuning: Tuning without an electronic tuner or app.

Remember with this method you may not be in tune with other instruments.

About Ukulele Tunings

The songs in this book were created for ukuleles tuned to standard C tuning using a High **G** (4th) string (C G E A).

This C tuning is the most common ukulele tuning and is the tuning most associated with the "ukulele sound". This C tuning is commonly referred to as C with a **"High G"** tuning because the **G** (4th) string has a higher pitch than the **C** (3rd) string.

Ukuleles are sometimes strung in C tuning with a lower pitch **G** (4th) string. This is known as C with a *"Low G"*. This tuning is similar to a standard guitar tuning.

DID YOU KNOW:
When you place a capo on the fifth fret of a 6-string guitar the first four guitar strings are the same pitch as Low G tuning on a ukulele. Playing a basic **D** chord on the guitar is equivalant to a **G** chord on the ukulele.

The *Baritone Ukulele* is tuned exactly like the last 4 strings of the guitar. D G B E.

Step 1. Tighten the **C** (3rd) string until you feel it sounds in pitch.

Step 2. Tune the **E** (2nd) string to the pitch of the **C** (3rd string).

Press your left index finger onto the fourth fret of the **C** string of your ukulele. This is an **E** note. Play the **E** note on the **C** string and then strike the open **E** string. Turn the **E** string until the notes of both strings sound the same.

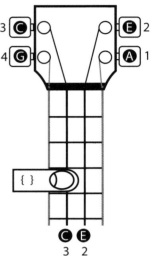

Step 3. Tune the **A** (1st) string to the pitch of the **E** (2nd) string.

Press your left index finger onto the fifth fret of the 2nd **E** string of your ukulele. This is an **A** note. Play the **A** note on the **E** string and then strike the open **A** (2nd) string. Turn the first string **A** until both strings sound the same.

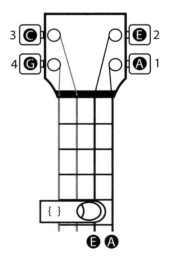

Step 4. Tune the High **G** (4th) string to the pitch of the **G** note on **E** (2nd) string.

Place your left index finger on the third fret of the **E** (2nd) string of your ukulele. This is a **G** note. Play the **G** note on the **E** (2nd) string and then strike the open **G** (4th) string. Both strings should sound the same. Turn the **G** (4th) string until both strings sound the same.

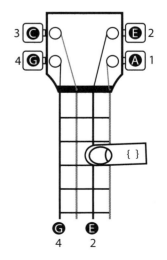

How to Read Tablature

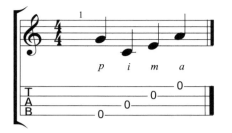

The songs in this book are written in both *Standard Music Notation* and *Ukulele Tablature.*

The diagram on the left shows the open strings of the Ukulele in *Standard Music notation* (top) and *Tablature* or *TAB* on the bottom. The lower case letters *p i m a* refer to the right hand fingers.

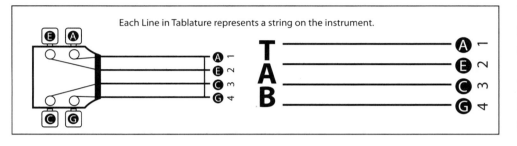

Tablature or *TAB* is system of music notation that tells you which string and fret to play. Each of the four staff lines represent a string on the ukulele. The numbers on each line (string) indicate which fret to press as the string is played.

The numbers on the lines indicate which fret to press down on that string. In the example to the right we see the number 3 indicated on the (A) string. Place your finger on the third fret of the (A) string and play that note.

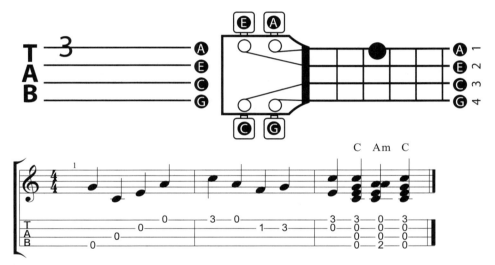

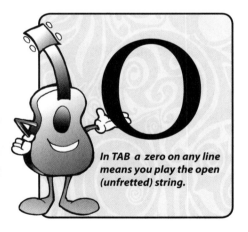

In TAB a zero on any line means you play the open (unfretted) string.

As is in classical music notation (above), we read TAB from left to right and use the vertical bars to organize the TAB notes into spaces called measures. When two or more numbers are stacked on top of each other those notes are played at the same time. Often chord names or diagrams are shown above TAB notes. **Remember: Play only the notes indicated in the TAB.**

The Secret Code of Tablature

The Pull-off

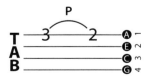

Place your 2nd finger (middle) on the third fret and your first finger on the second fret of the (A) (1st) string. Strike the (A) string and pull your 2nd finger (middle) off the string to create the second note. Strike the string one time only!

The Hammer-on

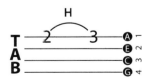

Place your 1st finger (index) on the second fret of the (A) (1st) string. Strike the (A) string and "hammer" your 2nd finger (middle) on the third fret to play the second note.

The Slide

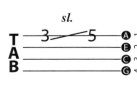

Place your 3rd finger (annular or ring finger) on the third fret of the (A) (1st) string. Strike the (A) string, press down on the fret and *slide your finger* from the 3rd to the 5th fret.

T'was the Night Before Christmas

Twas the night before Christmas,
when all through the house
Not a creature was stirring, not even a mouse.
The stockings were hung by the chimney with care,
In hopes that St Nicholas soon would be there.

The children were nestled all snug in their beds,
While visions of sugar-plums danced in their heads.
And mamma in her 'kerchief, and I in my cap,
Had just settled our brains for a long winter's nap.

When out on the lawn there arose such a clatter,
I sprang from the bed to see what was the matter.
Away to the window I flew like a flash,
Tore open the shutters and threw up the sash.

The moon on the breast of the new-fallen snow
Gave the lustre of mid-day to objects below.
When, what to my wondering eyes should appear,
But a miniature sleigh, and eight tinny reindeer.

With a little old driver, so lively and quick,
I knew in a moment it must be St Nick.
More rapid than eagles his coursers they came,
And he whistled, and shouted, and called them by name!

"Now Dasher! now, Dancer! now, Prancer and Vixen!
On, Comet! On, Cupid! on, on Donner and Blitzen!
To the top of the porch! to the top of the wall!
Now dash away! Dash away! Dash away all!"

As dry leaves that before the wild hurricane fly,
When they meet with an obstacle, mount to the sky.
So up to the house-top the coursers they flew,
With the sleigh full of Toys, and St Nicholas too.

And then, in a twinkling, I heard on the roof
The prancing and pawing of each little hoof.
As I drew in my head, and was turning around,
Down the chimney St Nicholas came with a bound.

He was dressed all in fur, from his head to his foot,
And his clothes were all tarnished with ashes and soot.
A bundle of Toys he had flung on his back,
And he looked like a peddler, just opening his pack.

His eyes-how they twinkled! his dimples how merry!
His cheeks were like roses, his nose like a cherry!
His droll little mouth was drawn up like a bow,
And the beard of his chin was as white as the snow.

The stump of a pipe he held tight in his teeth,
And the smoke it encircled his head like a wreath.
He had a broad face and a little round belly,
That shook when he laughed, like a bowlful of jelly!

He was chubby and plump, a right jolly old elf,
And I laughed when I saw him, in spite of myself!
A wink of his eye and a twist of his head,
Soon gave me to know I had nothing to dread.

He spoke not a word, but went straight to his work,
And filled all the stockings, then turned with a jerk.
And laying his finger aside of his nose,
And giving a nod, up the chimney he rose!

He sprang to his sleigh, to his team gave a whistle,
And away they all flew like the down of a thistle.
But I heard him exclaim, 'ere he drove out of sight,
"Happy Christmas to all, and to all a good-night!"

About the Author

KEV-Kevin Rones is a San Diego based Ukulele enthusiast, Harpguitarist and Fingerstyle Acoustic Guitarist. He is an author, illustrator, educator and acoustic performer, the founder of the San Diego Guitar Society, The School of Guitar Wizardry™ and The Acoustic Underground™ Concert Series.

His popular KEV's Quickstart™ Ukulele & Guitar method workshops continue to inspire and educate attendees.

For information on performances, products, booking, or to schedule a KEV Quickstart™ Workshop visit www.KEVmusic.com

KEV's Quickstart™
Fingerstyle Ukulele

A great companion book for Quickstart Ukulele Christmas Songs!

Available now! Ask for it at your local bookstore.
Order online and at bookstores and music stores near you.
ISBN 978-1-57424-278-2   SAN 683-8022

Fingerstyle Ukulele has become popular with Indie artists and emerging solo ukulele artists throughout the world. Fingerstyle ukulele combines picking patterns, chord strumming and melody lines to create interesting and fun arrangements.

This book will introduce you to the fundamentals of Fingerstyle Ukulele through a series of exersongs™ and arrangements created specifically for fingerstyle ukulele.

Try other KEV's Quickstart™ Products

Visit www.KEVmusic for more information on other KEV's Quickstart Products and workshops.

SPECIAL THANKS TO BARI ZWIRN whose encouragement and swift kick in the pants propelled me into teaching Ukulele. Bari is proof positive that good things indeed come in small packages!

More Great Christmas Books from Centerstream...

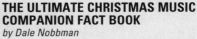